Little Inventions

GLASSES

RAPHAËL FEJTÖ

FIREFLY BOOKS

In the first century B.C., before glasses existed, it is said that Nero, a Roman emperor, held an emerald in front of his eyes to better see the gladiator fights.

We don't know if it actually worked, but no one would have dared contradict him.

At the same time, the Roman philosopher Seneca, who couldn't see very well, discovered that by holding a bowl filled with water in front of a text, he was able to read better.

Around 850, Abbas Ibn Firnas, a poet of Berber origin, had the idea of using a semi-precious cut stone. This worked even better than the bowl filled with water. It was the first magnifying device!

In 1268, an English monk read the scientific description of vision that was written by Alhazen, an Arab scientist, and decided to make the magnifying device... out of glass.

Then, the Italian physician Salvino Degli Armati decided to use glass from Murano, an island near Venice, because it was of excellent quality.

He created two wooden circles to surround the lenses, held together by a nail. These "nailed spectacles" were mostly used by doctors, monks and philosophers, since most people could not read.

Alessandro Della Spina, an Italian monk, decided to make a bunch of spectacles and distribute them for free on the streets, to the elderly and the poor.

However, these glasses only helped
people who couldn't read close up.

So, in 1440, glasses to correct myopia were invented: thanks to them, people could finally see very well from far away!

Back then, glasses didn't have arms and had to be balanced on the nose. Since they were very heavy, they often fell!

So, ribbons were attached so they could be tied behind the head. These glasses were very popular!

In 1728, English optician Edward Scarlett
replaced the ribbons with short arms that
rested against the temples.

But the arms had a big defect: they pressed hard against the temples and caused terrible headaches.

The middle class preferred a different type of glasses that had been invented: the *lorgnette*, a pair of glasses with a handle you had to hold. They were less practical, but at least they didn't cause headaches!

At the time, glasses blacksmiths
either mass produced or made
custom glasses.

Then traveling salesmen
started selling them.

In Spain, the richer someone was,
the bigger their glasses were.

In 1752, the English optician James Ayscough created the first pair of tinted glasses. But they weren't to protect your eyes from the sun: he believed that blue or green glass improved a person's vision!

Forty years later, Pierre-Hyacinthe Caseaux, a French master-ironworker, had the idea to twist the metal wire he used to make nails, so it would surround the lenses and create arms that would hook behind the ears.

These lightweight glasses were very popular. They were made in his shop and then sold in jewelry stores. At the time, there were no professional opticians.

In the 19th century, in England, dandies brought the monocle (single lens) into style because they thought it was more attractive than glasses.

In Europe, some people preferred the *pince-nez* ("pinch-nose"), a *lorgnette* without a handle, held by a spring on the nose.

Starting in 1950, frames were being made of plastic. This cost a lot less and the styles could be more varied, because plastic is a very flexible material.

So, overnight, everyone started wearing glasses to see better, but also... just to look fashionable!

Today, millions of glasses are sold around the world, and there are many different types!

sunglasses

eyeglasses

aviator glasses

swimming goggles

And you? Which are your favorite

GLASSES

?

There you go, now you know everything about the invention of GLASSES!

But do you remember everything you've read?

Play the MEMORY game to see what you remember!

MEMORY GAME

1. What did Emperor Nero use to better watch gladiator combats?

2. What material surrounded the lenses of the first glasses?

3. True or false: The first glasses didn't have any arms?

4. What do you call glasses with a handle?

5. In the past, in which type of stores could you buy glasses?

6. From which new material were frames made as of 1950?

1. An emerald.
2. Wood.
3. True.
4. The lorgnette.
5. In jewelry stores.
6. Plastic.

A FIREFLY BOOK

Published by Firefly Books Ltd. 2016

Source edition © 2015 Les Lunettes, ÉDITIONS PLAY BAC, 33 rue du Petit-Musc, 75004, Paris, France, 2015

This translated edition copyright © 2016 Firefly Books

First printing

Publisher Cataloging-in-Publication Data (U.S.)

Names: Fejtö, Raphaël, author. | Greenspoon, Golda, translator. | Mersereau, Claudine, translator.
Title: Glasses / Raphaël Fejtö.
Description: Richmond Hill, Ontario, Canada : Firefly Books, 2016. | Series: Little Inventions | Originally published by Éditions Play Bac, Paris, 2015 as Les p'tites inventions: La Lunettes | Summary: "This brief history on one of the small, overlooked inventions we use in our everyday lives, in a six-part series is geared toward children. With fun and quirky illustrations and dialog, it also comes with a memory quiz to ensure children retain what they learn" -- Provided by publisher.
Identifiers: ISBN 978-1-77085-747-6 (hardcover)
Subjects: LCSH: Eyeglasses -- Juvenile literature. | Eyeglasses -- History – Juvenile literature.
Classification: LCC RE976.F458 |DDC 617.522 – dc23

Library and Archives Canada Cataloguing in Publication

Fejtö, Raphaël
[Lunettes. English]
     Glasses / Raphaël Fejtö.
(Little inventions)
Translation of: Les lunettes.
ISBN 978-1-77085-747-6 (bound)
        1. Eyeglasses--History--Juvenile literature. I. Title.
II. Title: Lunettes. English.
RE971.F4613 2016   j617.7'522   C2016-900075-3

Published in the United States by
Firefly Books (U.S.) Inc.
P.O. Box 1338, Ellicott Station
Buffalo, New York 14205

Published in Canada by
Firefly Books Ltd.
50 Staples Avenue, Unit 1
Richmond Hill, Ontario L4B 0A7

Printed in China

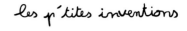